HAL LEONARD
BAGPIPE METHOD

BAGPIPE METHOD

BY RON BOWEN AND SARAJANE TRIER

ISBN 978-1-4768-1344-8

HAL•LEONARD®

Visit Hal Leonard Online at
www.halleonard.com

Contact us:
Hal Leonard
7777 West Bluemound Road
Milwaukee, WI 53213
Email: info@halleonard.com

In Europe, contact:
Hal Leonard Europe Limited
42 Wigmore Street
Marylebone, London, W1U 2RN
Email: info@halleonardeurope.com

In Australia, contact:
Hal Leonard Australia Pty. Ltd.
4 Lentara Court
Cheltenham, Victoria, 3192 Australia
Email: info@halleonard.com.au

CONTENTS

INTRODUCTION

When played with proficiency, the Great Highland Bagpipe (GHB) can awaken a range of emotions that otherwise remain hidden or dormant. As an instrument in battle, it has been known to spirit warriors to victory despite great disadvantage. As an instrument of celebration, generations have danced and tapped their toes to the intricate rhythms and complexities of jigs, reels, and hornpipes. Few can resist the more melancholy notes of a hymn, slow air, or ancient piobaireachd (*Piobaireachd, pibroch, or ceol mor* is an art music genre associated primarily with the Scottish Highlands.)

"To the make of a piper go seven years... at the end of his seven years one born to it will stand at the start of knowledge, and leaning a fond ear to the drone he may have parley with old folks of old affairs." – Neil Munro

In the early stages, rapid progress can be made on the Great Highland Bagpipe, but as with most instruments, mastery is very difficult. Some say the GHB is the most difficult instrument in the world to master. Those who have previous experience or expertise with other instruments will enjoy little advantage over those without. This book will focus on techniques and skills required to produce simple melodies. The learning will be done on a practice chanter, whose fingering is identical to that of a full-size bagpipe.

Our goal is to provide learners with basic and essential skills. Our method will allow for an early transition to the full instrument, the Great Highland Bagpipe. While playing simple tunes on a practice chanter will come easily, playing a bagpipe can be a daunting experience. Nothing about it is easy. If one is committed to learning the instrument, we recommend the early purchase of a suitable instrument. In our experience as teachers of hundreds of teenagers and adults, with the methods and music covered within this book, skill development is rapid and one can expect to be "parade worthy" in two to six months. Beyond this, with hard work and personal instruction, becoming a competition piper at the highest level is possible.

This tutor is a collaborative effort between two musicians, Sarajane Trier and me, Ron Bowen. Sarajane was educated as a musician. She was drawn to the bagpipe and found considerable difficulty in understanding the instrument, its music, and the accepted teaching methods. Like many pipers, I have only ever played one instrument. I was a late starter and broke most of the rules in order to hasten my progress. I was fortunate to play in some outstanding bands and later to build some very successful competition bagpipe bands. This tutor employs the very best from two distinctly different perspectives. It will lessen the initial pain and drudgery generally associated with learning the bagpipe and it will accelerate your progress onto the pipes, to more challenging music, and beyond.

ABOUT THE AUTHORS

Ron Bowen is a second-generation piper who began this particular journey at the relatively old age of 20. Within 18 months of starting he had secured a spot in a top level Grade One pipe band, the Waterloo Regional Police Pipe Band in Ontario, Canada. "Ringo," as he is known to his friends, spent the next 30 years playing in and leading various competition bands throughout Ontario before accepting a full-time bagpipe teaching assignment in the United States. Ron wrote, published, and sold a book worldwide entitled *The Care and Maintenance of the Great Highland Bagpipe*. He also maintains the largest online museum of antique bagpipes at **www.thebagpipeplace.com**. In addition to being in demand worldwide regarding the identification and restoration of vintage bagpipes, Ron continues to play, instruct, and conduct workshops.

Sarajane Trier studied music at Carroll University in Waukesha, Wisconsin where she attended a Bagpipe Master's Class (recital and information session) on the instrument at age 18. She kept bagpipes on her bucket list while building a 25-year career in real estate and finance. In 2004 (at age 40), she acted on her passion and quickly fell victim to the complications and complexities of learning this challenging instrument. In 2005, she attended a week-long piping workshop and her understanding and proficiency took a dramatic turn for the better. Over the next several years, Sarajane became a competing piper, a principle teacher of three pipe bands and many individuals throughout Wisconsin, and a bagpipe and drumming instructor at a private school. Ms. Trier is the owner/operator of the MidWest School of Piping and Drumming, currently maintains **www.thebagpipeschool.com**, and is very much in demand as a performer and instructor.

PREAMBLE TO LEARNING

The essence of playing the Great Highland Bagpipe is twofold:

1) One must have a proper and tuned instrument
2) One must be able to present a pleasing melody

This all sounds quite simple; however, it is anything but simple. Learning to blow a bagpipe properly is a daunting task. Playing a melody (on a recorder-like instrument called a practice chanter) is relatively simple, however, it becomes more and more complicated with demanding finger embellishments, which we will discuss later.

Age has its advantages and disadvantages. You don't have to begin lessons at age 14 in order to become an excellent piper. At the same time, you don't have to be an adult to advance quickly on the bagpipes and be able to play tunes. The learning methods presented herein have proven successful with students of all ages and abilities. In the broadest of terms, bagpipes are not taught, they are learned. The student's natural ability, determination, work ethic, aptitude, and attitude will all be major determining factors in both the speed at which one learns and the level of proficiency to which one will ascend. Learning bagpipes correctly is about building a solid foundation of fundamental skills and understanding. It does little good to teach difficult and complicated movements if students are not going to be able to apply these correctly within the context of the music played.

Learning bagpipes is an extremely broad topic. Typically, most of what is learned is done so by rote, without fully understanding what the finished product is supposed to be. Most of the attention is focused on specific tasks. Once mastered, specific skills are linked together and woven into complex musical melodies. Again, it has been said that the Great Highland Bagpipe is the most difficult musical instrument to master. Its music is a total and complete expression of the musician—physically, mentally, and emotionally.

It has been said that seven years go to the making of a piper, and seven generations go before the seven years. I wish that it was so simple.

Adults are blessed with higher powers of reasoning and greater physical strength, however, in terms of the Great Highland Bagpipe, they are disadvantaged in just about every other respect. Fingers lack the accuracy and dexterity of younger hands. Musical concepts form slowly and years of negative programming block progress.

The challenges of learning bagpipes as an adult are only partly the fault of the adult. Traditional teaching methods handed down, generation after generation, are biased towards youthful students. These methods applied to adult learners impede progress, deny the pleasure and reward of accomplishment, and ultimately arrest individuals far beneath their potential. What we will present herein are concepts and strategies that are intended to accelerate, if not revolutionize, adult learning of the bagpipe.

The music of the Great Highland Bagpipe is broken down into two primary components—sound and melody. Together they create something majestic and stirring.

Ron Bowen as Pipe Major of Niagara Regional Police Pipe Band

Sound is all about the production of complimentary harmonic tones that remain perfectly in tune with each other throughout the musical performance. A piper must understand his or her instrument in a way that no other musician can comprehend. A piper must understand and eventually master every aspect of the production of correct bagpipe sound.

Melody is all about the presentation of musical notes arranged in a rhythmic and pleasing manner. Understanding this will strip away many false pretenses and allow students to progress to the point where they are a credit to the instrument, the music, and to themselves.

As I said earlier, the music of the GHB is harmonic tones and melody. A melody is an arrangement of notes that is rhythmic and pleasing. If your imagination will allow it, a melody tells a story, or sings a song. A good melody will invite, accommodate, and generate emotion, both within the piper and within the audience.

Soon after the student learns the scale, most teachers will now spend months or years teaching embellishments. Embellishments are grace notes, doublings, grips, and other complicated note couplings. Embellishments are integral to the music and offer very important aspects of articulation, accent, and rhythm. Interestingly, none of these are necessary in order to present the melody of a tune. The sole purpose of embellishments is to enhance the melody by adding rhythmic differences to a melodic line.

I wanted to break up this paragraph because we are about to jump on a thin spot of the ice...

The essence of good music is careful and heartfelt expression and interpretation, the combination of accurate finger placement, correct tempo, rhythmic accuracy, and the rhythmic support of the melodic line with proper embellishments. This sounds so easy. Of these, rhythmic accuracy might be the most important. Therefore, embellishments not played in the correct rhythm will hurt rather than help or enhance the melodic line.

If one accepts this premise, one must wonder why so many learners and their teachers persist in inserting embellishments to the detriment of all else. I believe that in many instances the focus is so great on embellishments that both sound and melody suffer incomprehensibly. Yet, this method of teaching continues.

By no means am I minimizing the importance of embellishments or suggesting that they should not be taught or learned. They should, however, be placed in context with the student and his or her abilities. And they should not be placed in a position of importance higher than either sound or melody.

Ron Bowen, Pipe Major and Principal Instructor of Braemar Pipe Bands, St. Catharines
One Hundred Pipers and Drummers, Three Competing Pipe Bands, Two North American Championships

A proper melody is played at a steady tempo. Note placement is respectful of "the beat" and this is maintained throughout the tune. Once you teach this, embellishments can be added in and bolted on within the abilities of the student without sacrificing either sound or melody!

So, learners! If I told you that if you start today and practice a half hour each day for the next three months, you'll be able to play simple street tunes with your band on parade and be absolutely rock solid in sound and also playing the melody "on the beat," what would you say? I thought so! Let's get started.

This approach to teaching is based on over 40 years of experience as a competitive piper, pipe major, and as a professional bagpipe instructor. If you would indulge me for just a minute further, I have witnessed those who have been piping for many years who are not capable of producing the right sound, or playing a simple melody to a steady beat, or at a pleasing tempo. Their effort to put in every doubling and every grip causes them to distort the feeling of the tune and the music of their instrument.

Braemar Pipeband

On the other hand, I have taken these same individuals and explained the concepts written herein. At first there is shock and disbelief. This soon gives way to relief and renewed enthusiasm. Soon they are playing simple tunes on the beat and up to tempo. Embellishments are added, in keeping with the student's ability to maintain timing, tempo, and focus on producing the correct sound.

In closing, this method is also acceptable for younger learners who might otherwise lose interest and not progress using traditional teaching methods. If the student wishes to pursue a higher level of competence, additional effort and dedication regarding embellishments will need to take place. Regardless, the methods explained herein help form a strong foundation upon which all else rests.

The Boys from St. John's Northwestern Military Academy at the Cinco de Mayo Parade in Puebla, Mexico

THE PRACTICE CHANTER

You will need a practice chanter. You should be paying somewhere between $60 and $100 for a suitable practice chanter and reed. Make your purchase from a reputable dealer or maker. Do your homework. I recommend that you limit your search to makers in North America or the UK.

With the reed properly inserted in the chanter and blown at the correct pressure, the practice chanter will produce a modestly irritating sound. Blow too little and the chanter will growl and quack. Blow too hard and it may squeal and/or cease sounding altogether. Find that "happy place" in between and blow your chanter that way always.

Your chanter has one note-hole on the backside, and seven note-holes on the front. Your fingers will cover all note-holes to produce low G.

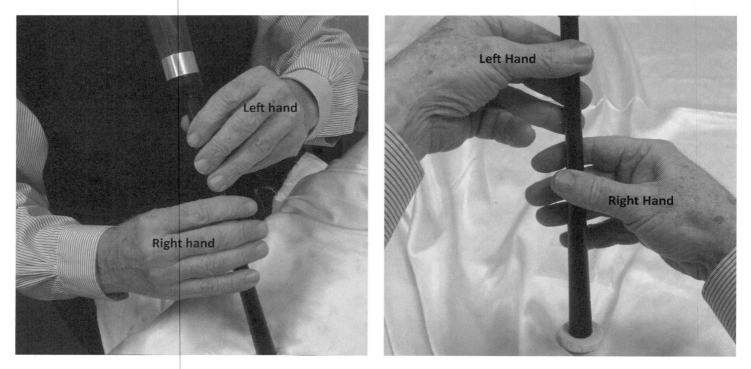

Your left hand goes on top and your right hand goes on the bottom. Let's start by putting the thumb of your left hand over the hole on the back of the chanter. Blow into your chanter. You can hear different notes when you open and cover the hole intermittently.

Do not try to cover the hole with the flat of your thumb. Use the top side of your thumb (as in the pictures above) so that when your fingers are placed over the holes in the front of the chanter, they will feel natural and relaxed.

Now refer to the front of your chanter. Cover the top three holes using your index, middle, and ring fingers. Your pinky will remain unused. Now place the pinky on your right hand over the bottom-most hole. Keeping your fingers relaxed; place them gently on the chanter, each finger covering a note-hole in succession. Your thumb will rest gently on the backside of the chanter as shown in the picture above. Note that you are not using your fingertips. There are good reasons for this. When we play the various notes on a chanter, we lift our fingers straight up rather than curl them back. This allows a piper to move his or her fingers very quickly with great accuracy. This is not possible using fingertips.

Look at the pictures above. This is the proper way to hold a practice chanter. Once again, note that the fingers are across the chanter. Do not play with your fingertips! Hold the practice chanter gently but securely. Rest the bottom edge of the base of the practice chanter on a table. Keep your elbows up and your wrists straight.

THE GREAT HIGHLAND BAGPIPE SCALE

Now let's look at the correct finger placement for each note. Your fingers should remain relaxed and relatively straight across the chanter. Here are the first three notes of the scale.

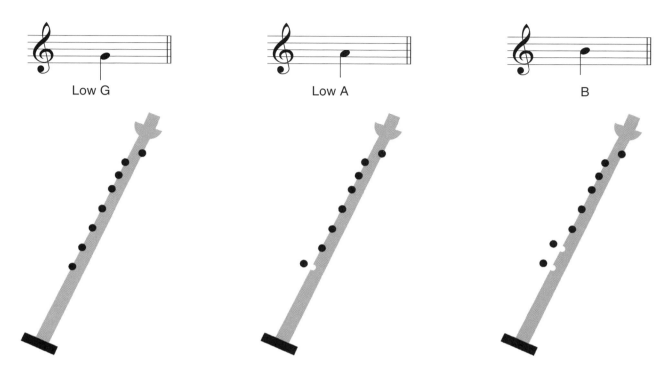

Low G   Low A   B

METRONOMES

Buy a good metronome and use it *always*. As a matter of fact, we want you to walk, talk, blink, and think to the beat! You can't do this without using your metronome. Don't kid yourself and think that you can keep time with your foot. You'll just end up tapping your foot to your fingers and develop a false sense of timing!

When you see the video symbol, go to the video and watch the lesson. Practice the lessons and compare your playing to these references. Now, go ahead and watch the video introduction.

INTRO

Staff notation tells us everything we need to know about how something is to be played. We're not going to go into this in detail at this point, however you should know some basic information right from the beginning.

1) The exercise below is written in *4/4 time.* This means that there are four beats to a *measure* and that each *quarter note* (1/4 note) gets a beat. I'm going to ask you to play every quarter note exactly on each beat. (See more on *time signatures* in the Understanding Bagpipe Notation section.)

2) The small notes are called *grace notes.* Grace notes are played to accent or embellish a *melody* note (a regular, non-grace note). Remember, there are no *dynamics* with bagpipes. We play at one volume only. Grace notes and other embellishments are our only way of introducing additional interest and ornamentation to the music. In the notation above, these are G grace notes. The G grace note is played by lifting only your index finger and placing it back down over the note-hole very quickly and with some conviction. Refer to Video Lesson 1 to see the correct technique for playing this grace note.

3) The curved line above two or more identical notes is called a *tie.* This connects notes to be played as a single tone. In this instance, each quarter note receives one beat. Listen to and watch the sound clip for Video Lesson 1 to understand how it is to be played.

Set your metronome to a comfortable speed for this exercise. Initially, it might be about 50 beats per minute. Increase the speed as your competence grows, however, the goal here is to play each note on the beat. Remember, in a 4/4 tune, each quarter note receives a beat and there are four beats per measure.

LESSON 1

The pictures below represent the next three notes. They involve a change from bottom hand to top hand. Carefully practice the transition between notes. Make sure there are no crossing noises!

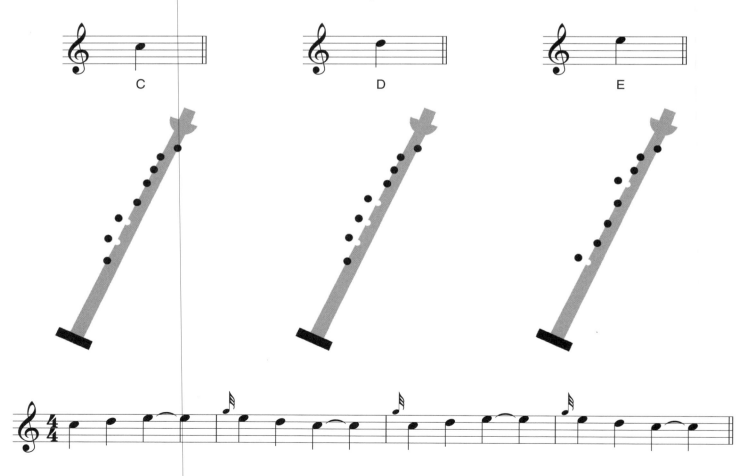

LESSON 2

Video Lesson 2 is simply a continuation of the scale. It involves both the bottom hand and top hand. When transitioning from a bottom hand note to a top hand note, and vice versa, make sure there are not crossing noises. Make a clean transition. Move slowly and carefully. It's far easier to maintain good habits than to correct bad habits.

REPETITION & MUSCLE MEMORY

Repetition is the key to success. Practice these exercises over and over. This will create "muscle memory," in which your fingers will move simply at the sight of a note and without cognitive process.

The last three notes are all top hand notes. It takes a little practice to go from high G to high A correctly. Study the pictures and the video and practice this carefully.

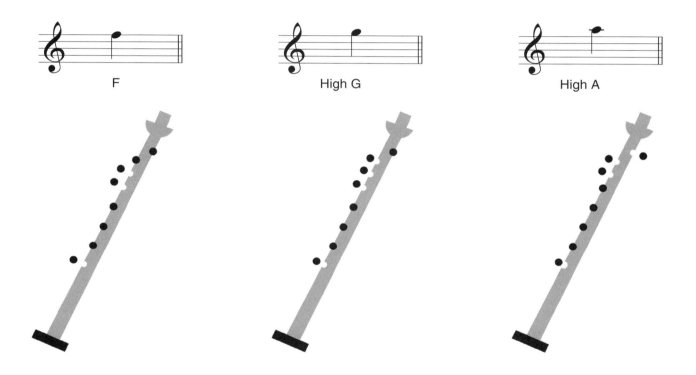

F   High G   High A

LESSON 3

Look at the exercise below. Now here's a switch! We're still playing a G grace note, however, when you play it from high A, the approach is very different. Rather than using your index finger to play the G grace note, just brush your thumb across the high A note-hole. The result is a G grace note from high A, commonly called a "thumb grace note."

Okay! So there we have the nine notes that make up the scale for the Great Highland Bagpipe. That wasn't so bad. Now let's put all nine together.

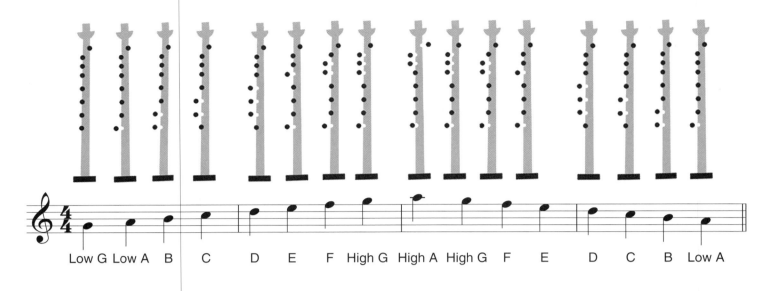

| Low G | Low A | B | C | D | E | F | High G | High A | High G | F | E | D | C | B | Low A |

Practice the scale to your metronome. Accuracy is the goal. Only increase the speed of your metronome as you are able to do so without sacrificing quality.

NOTE NAMES

The scale above is shown with the corresponding note name directly below the note. This is a reference only and is intended to help you to associate the note with its name. Do not write the alphabetic note name on any sheet music. It only provides part of the information you need and will only slow you down.

Note: If you've played other instruments before, you'll probably recognize that the notes C and F on the bagpipes are actually the notes C♯ and F♯! But since the natural versions of C and F are not commonly played on the bagpipes, it has become accepted practice to simply drop the sharp symbol when referring to these notes, even though they actually sound as C♯ and F♯.

FIRST EXERCISE

Now that we've gotten our fingers around the nine notes that make up the GHB scale, let's take on something just a bit more challenging. The following exercise is a great way to build finger coordination. It may seem difficult at first. Set your metronome at about 40 beats per minute. Work on this exercise one measure at a time. Go over and over each measure until it becomes natural. Then link all the measures together to play the entire exercise. Note that in the last measure, I've used a *half note*. It has the same value as two tied quarter notes.

LESSON 4

Here's the exercise above. Remember, speed is not a substitute for accuracy or correctness. Push yourself to play the exercise at faster tempos, however, not to the point where execution starts to fail. If you hear or feel your technique failing, hold the line at that speed for a few days before trying a faster tempo.

G, D, AND E GRACE NOTES

The music of the Great Highland Bagpipe is comprised of a melody played on a chanter against a background of harmony provided by three drones. Since there are only nine notes, we embellish notes to provide articulation and accent, creating "color" and additional interest to the music. Embellishments range from a single grace note to strings of grace notes played as a single movement.

Embellishments are played distinctly and with considerable conviction. They should be consistently perfect, both technically and musically. The finished product should be exciting to witness. Embellishments should always be played in context with the music and should never receive attention at the expense of the sound of our instrument or the melody and consistent tempo of the music being played. We'll take a magnifying glass to these words later.

Let's look at the exercise below. You will see G, D, and E grace notes associated with specific melody notes. Aha! This is a great time to mention that all embellishments are associated with the melody note immediately following the embellishment! Here, our melody note is low A.

GRACE NOTE TECHNIQUE

A grace note is played by lifting *one finger* briefly and returning it to the chanter. For instance, a G grace note is played by lifting the index finger of your top hand for a fraction of a second and placing it back on the chanter. An E grace note is played by doing the same with your ring finger on the top hand. And a D grace note is played by lifting only the index finger of your bottom hand.

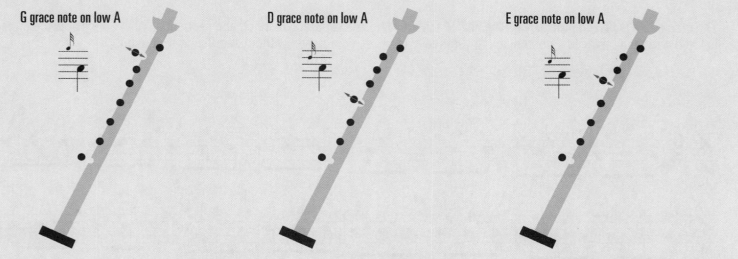

Focus on returning your finger to the chanter with a strong and forceful movement. The sound should be short, solid, and crisp to help emphasize the melody note that follows. **Note:** When playing with a metronome, if a single grace note is attached to a melody note, the grace note is played directly on the beat, not before.

BREATHING

There are no rests in bagpipe music. Often musicians use rests or phrasing marks to budget their breath while producing a melody. However, once a bagpipe is going, you can't shut it off until the tune, or set, is complete. (This is where the "bag" comes into play with the "pipe"). Therefore, you must develop the skill of breathing with a practice chanter to accommodate learning the music as you'll play it on the full bagpipe.

Beginners often try to play an exercise or tune without stopping for air. With this instrument you must take a breath when you need one. Phrasing is accomplished differently than what you may have learned on another wind instrument.

To do this, have your fingers play all of the notes and do not stop them when you need to take a breath. It will seem very odd at first, but eventually you'll become accustomed to playing and occasionally not hearing the notes your fingers are playing. Once you transition to the GHB, this will make infinitely more sense!

You will encounter G, D, and E grace notes countless times in bagpipe music. You'll see them as single grace notes, as G–D–E triplets, and incorporated into other embellishments (in whole and in part). Simply stated, you can't practice G–D–E grace-note exercises too much. Having said that, let's tackle the following exercises.

PLAYING TIP

Grace notes within bagpipe music are played precisely on the beat. In effect, they "borrow" time from the value of the melody note they precede. This is critical in order to achieve unison when playing with one or more pipers.

The grace note is played precisely on the beat. Each grace note is separate, distinct, and sequential. Also notice how the finger is lifted and then replaced with conviction. Gradually increase your speed without sacrificing execution.

This is a little busier than we're used to. The time signature here is 6/8, which means that there are six beats to a measure and that each *eighth note* (1/8 note) gets a beat. If we set our metronome at about 120 beats per minute and play each note on the beat, it will sound something like this. **Remember:** separate – distinct – sequential.

Practice them over and over until you're nailing each note on the beat. Many pipers do not understand or play G–D–E movements correctly, primarily because they've never been taught correctly! In one simple explanation, each note is distinct, played in the correct sequence of G–D–E, and the emphasis is in placing the finger onto the chanter, not in lifting the finger from the chanter.

Listen to the same G–D–E movement played a bit faster. Listen to how the individual notes are precise and played with both separation and strength. Learning to play the G–D–E movement like this will improve grace-noting, doublings, *toarluths*, and general technique.

LESSON 5

UNDERSTANDING BAGPIPE NOTATION

We're almost ready to start our first tune! First we have to learn how to read staff notation. Music is its own language made up of differing sounds of varying duration arranged in a melodic rhythm. Bagpipe music was originally passed on through oral tradition. Notes and embellishments were assigned their own words, which were sung. In this manner, tunes were passed on from teacher to student for hundreds of years. During the 18th century, great effort was put forward to preserve the music through translation into staff notation.

The following explanation of how to read music is intended to get you through the initial stages of learning only. Students at an advanced level are expected to understand staff notation in greater detail, sight-read, and write music.

THE STAFF

Music is written on a *staff*. A staff is comprised of five lines and four spaces. Notes are written either on a line or in a space. Because the high A is above the staff, it is written on a *ledger line*.

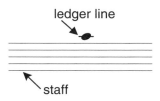

At the beginning of every line of music is the information that we need in order to correctly interpret the music. The *treble clef* is used exclusively in all bagpipe music, as we only have nine notes. The *time signature* is indicated by two numbers which is explained on the next page.

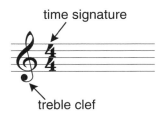

Notes are arranged in phrases and are contained within a *measure*. A vertical bar called a *bar line* separates measures. A *double bar line* indicates the end of a section of music. Measures contained within bar lines with two colons, called *repeat signs*, indicate that they are to be repeated in sequence before proceeding to the next part of the tune.

TIME SIGNATURES

Time signatures (or *meters*) define the pulse of the music by indicating the number of beats per measure. There are two types of time signatures: *simple time* and *compound time*.

The most common simple time signatures are 2/4, 3/4, and 4/4. The top number indicates the number of beats per measure, while the bottom number references the kind of note receiving one beat. For example, in 2/4 time there are two beats per measure and the quarter note receives one full beat (you'll learn more about note values in the following section). Again, in this example, you are likely to encounter two groupings of notes within a measure, each totaling one quarter (1/4) in note value. The beat lands on the first note of the grouping.

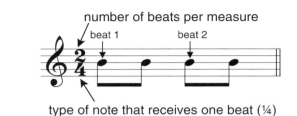

I like to offer the concept of "how many of what" when explaining time signatures. In the instance of 2/4, we know that there are two beats per bar with each count being a quarter note. Similarly in 3/4, we know that there are three beats per bar with each beat being a quarter note.

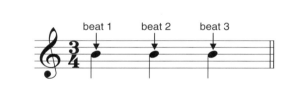

In compound time, again, the top number indicates the number of beats per bar and the bottom number indicates the kind of note receiving one beat. In compound time, the eighth note represents a single beat. In bagpipe music, we group beats together to correspond to marching tempos.

6/8, 9/8, and 12/8 are all considered compound time. In a 6/8 march, we group our eighth notes in two groups of three. When marching, we play the first group of three eighth notes on the left foot and the second group of three eighth notes on the right foot.

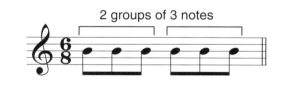

The easiest way to understand compound time for marching tunes is to divide the top number by three to give you the number of steps per bar. Each step (or pulse) will contain three notes of the value indicated.

This explanation will suffice for the time being. We will revisit this later, however, let's now turn our attention to note values before we get into our first tune.

NOTE VALUES

Note value is very simple to understand. The duration of the whole note is determined by the tempo. A whole note played at a slower tempo will be longer in duration than a whole note played at a faster tempo. It's really just a mathematical equation.

For example, if we are playing a tune where each quarter note was held for two seconds, an eighth note would be held for one second and a sixteenth note would be held for one half second.

Here's a breakdown of note values:

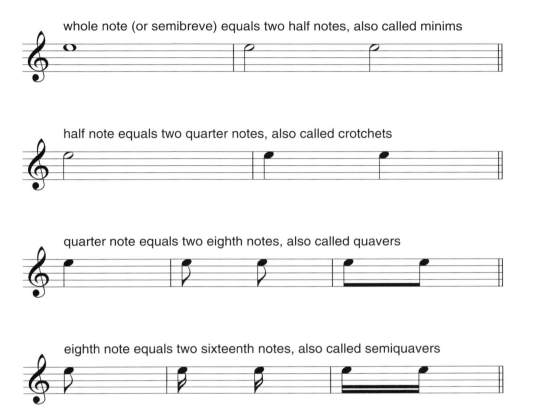

Notes are sometimes coupled together (or *beamed* together) when they share a beat. The beat will always fall on the first note of a coupling.

Notes can be expressed by symbol, numeric symbol, and both the American and United Kingdom terminology:

American	United Kingdom	Numeric Symbol	Symbol
whole note	semibreve	1	𝅝
half note	minim	1/2	𝅗𝅥
quarter note	crotchet	1/4	𝅘𝅥
eighth note	quaver	1/8	𝅘𝅥𝅮
sixteenth note	semiquaver	1/16	𝅘𝅥𝅯
thirty-second note	demisemiquaver	1/32	𝅘𝅥𝅰

Here's another way to think about note values. Let's say that "1" is the beginning of the sounded note. In a 4/4 tune, a whole note would sound for four beats. A half note would sound for two beats, a quarter note would sound for one beat, and an eighth note would sound for a half beat. This is visually expressed in the diagram below.

A *flag* (or *tail*) is used to cut the value of notes smaller than a quarter note in half. For instance, a quarter note has no flag. One flag indicates that the value of the note is an eighth, two flags indicate that the value is a sixteenth, and three flags indicate that the value is a thirty-second.

If the grey color is "sound," we see that the quarter note is heard for one beat, the half note is heard for two beats, and the whole note is heard for four beats. In the lower diagram, the shortest sound is the thirty-second note. The sixteenth note is heard for one quarter of the beat and the eighth note is heard for one half of the beat.

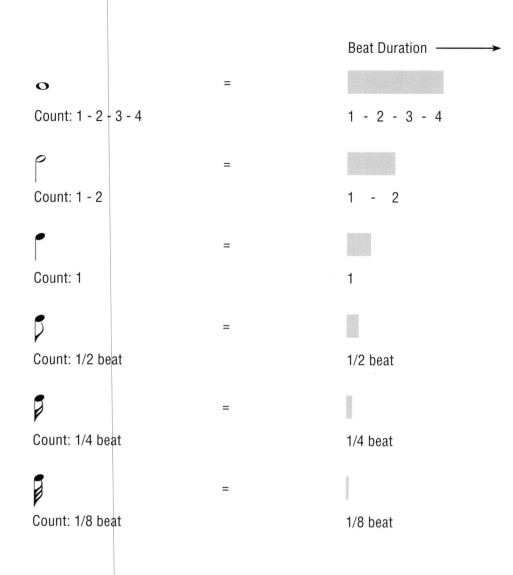

Beat Duration ⟶

𝅝	=	
Count: 1 - 2 - 3 - 4		1 - 2 - 3 - 4
𝅗𝅥	=	
Count: 1 - 2		1 - 2
𝅘𝅥	=	
Count: 1		1
𝅘𝅥𝅮	=	
Count: 1/2 beat		1/2 beat
𝅘𝅥𝅯	=	
Count: 1/4 beat		1/4 beat
𝅘𝅥𝅰	=	
Count: 1/8 beat		1/8 beat

One way to learn how to read music better is to simply take a tune and break it down note by note. Go through and identify each note's value and where they are relative to the primary beats within the bar.

If we set our metronome at a "reasonable" tempo of 84 beats per minute, we can count the various notes within each measure. In the first measure, we have a whole note which sounds for all four beats. The second measure has two half notes, each sounding for two beats. The third measure has four quarter notes, each sounding for one beat. Finally, we have the last measure with couplings of eighth notes. These are counted as "one and two and three and four and."

Count: 1 - 2 - 3 - 4   1 - 2   3 - 4   1   2   3   4   1 & 2 & 3 & 4 &

OUR FIRST TUNE — "BLUE BELLS OF SCOTLAND"

"Blue Bells of Scotland" is an old folk song which, like many, has multiple versions springing from different eras. Most historians agree that the song began as the poetry of a woman named Anne MacVicar Grant. Anne was born in 1755. In 1801, she was widowed with eight children and sought to support herself and her children by publishing poems she had written over the years.

We've chosen "Blue Bells of Scotland" as our first tune with good reason: it is written mostly with quarter notes, four to a measure. Also, the first line of music is essentially the same as the second and fourth lines. You really only have to learn two lines of music to play the entire tune!

Not quite so fast. Before we do, we have to learn a new embellishment! It's called a *D throw* or a *throw on D*.

There are different versions of the D throw, generally represented by the symbol to the right. We could spend the next chapter discussing this embellishment in its various forms, however we won't. Instead we're going to learn the simplest variation and apply it to "Blue Bells of Scotland."

LESSON 6

On the right is the simplified or "light" D throw. Here is how to play it. We're going to go from any preceding melody note directly to D as it is normally played. Then, very quickly, we're going to tap your bottom hand index finger down onto the chanter to sound C followed by the D melody note. It's really quite simple. Practice the following exercise.

In order to play "Blue Bells of Scotland" correctly we must play grace note embellishments, the light throw on D, and an embellishment called a *strike*.

A strike is simply two identical notes that are separated by a grace note. The example on the left is an E strike off of F, and the example on the right is an A strike off of E. See Video Lesson 7 for details. In tunes with a quick tempo, the strike is made quickly with a quick touch of one or more fingers.

Go to the video and watch how a strike is played. Practice the strikes above slowly and accurately.

LESSON 7

If we work ourselves through the first few measures, we start off with a half note which consumes two beats. It is followed by two quarter notes, each consuming one beat. But before we leave the first measure, let's look at the F grace note following the high A half note and immediately before the high G quarter note. This is played by sounding high A, moving to F for a split second, before resting on high G for the duration of the beat.

Later you'll see a low G grace note, which is called a low G strike. This is played by simply closing the chanter for a moment before opening it to the next melody note.

This tune also features a new type of note called a *dotted note*. Just as a flag will reduce the value of a note by one half, adding a *dot* immediately after a note increases its value by one half. For example, adding a dot to a quarter note increases the note value to one and a half beats. Adding a dot to a half note will lengthen its value to three beats.

NOTATION TIP

Again, think of a note as consuming time within a measure. A whole note will consume the entire time within the measure. A smaller note will consume only a portion of what a whole note will consume.

BLUE BELLS OF SCOTLAND

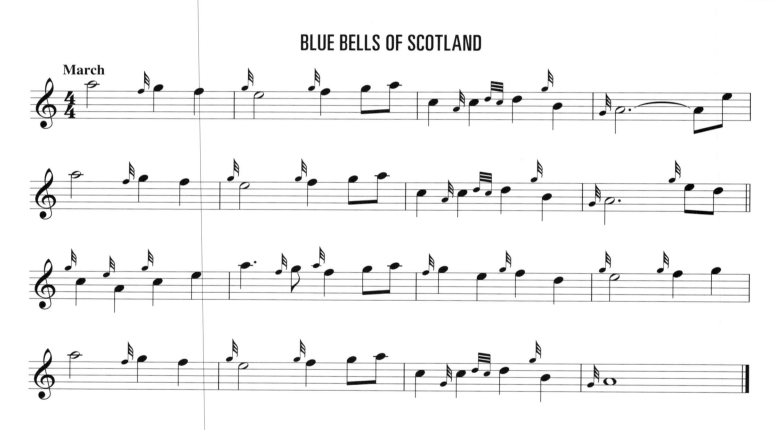

Aha! I slipped in a new embellishment! In the second measure of the second part (measure 10) is a high A grace note, most often called a thumb grace note. In this instance, we're transitioning from a high G melody note to an F melody note. But just before we play F, we're taking all our top hand fingers off the chanter for a split second before putting our thumb and index finger over the note-holes to sound F. Review Video Lesson 6 carefully for help on this.

Why did we choose "Blue Bells?" Look at the first, second, and fourth lines. They're all *very* similar! It's a great example of a simple melody arranged into a beautiful tune. Let's not stop here. Let's learn another tune!

OUR SECOND TUNE —
"STAR OF THE COUNTY DOWN"

Our next tune is absolutely lovely. The melody dates back to at least 1707, when it was published as "Dives and Lazarus." The lyrics were added sometime in the 20th century by Cathal McGarvey. Whether one plays this tune as a slow air or up-tempo as a march, it has a haunting melody that evokes considerable emotion. Let's look at the lyrics first, and the tune follows.

Star of the County Down

In Banbridge town in the County Down
One morning last July,
From a boreen green came a sweet Colleen
And she smiled as she passed me by.
She looked so sweet from her two bare feet
To the sheen of her nut brown hair.
Such a coaxing elf, sure I shook myself
For to see I was really there.

Chorus:
From Bantry Bay up to Derry Quay and
From Galway to Dublin town,
No maid I've seen like the brown Colleen
That I met in the County Down.

As she onward sped, sure I scratched my head,
And I looked with a feelin' rare
And I says, says I, to a passerby
"Whose the maid with the nut brown hair?"
He smiled at me and he says, says he,
"That's the gem of Ireland's crown.
It's Rosie McCann from the banks of Bann,
She's the star of the County Down."

She'd a soft brown eye and a look so sly,
And a smile like the rose in June,
And you hung on each note from her lily-white throat,
As she lilted an Irish tune.
At the pattern dance you were held in a trance,
As she tripped through a reel or a jig;
And when her eyes she'd roll, she'd coax, on my soul,
A spud from a hungry pig.

(repeat Chorus)

I've traveled a bit, but I never was hit
Since my roving career began;
But fair and square I surrendered there
To the charms of young Rose McCann.
I'd a heart to let and no tenant yet
Though I'd searched countryside and town;
But in she went, and I asked no rent
From the Star of the County Down.

(repeat Chorus)

At the Harvest Fair she'll be surely there
And I'll dress in my Sunday clothes,
With my shoes shone bright and my hat cocked right
For a smile from my nut brown rose.
No pipe I'll smoke, no horse I'll yoke
Till my plough turns rust coloured brown.
Till a smiling bride, by my own fireside
Sits the star of the County Down.

(repeat Chorus)

STAR OF THE COUNTY DOWN

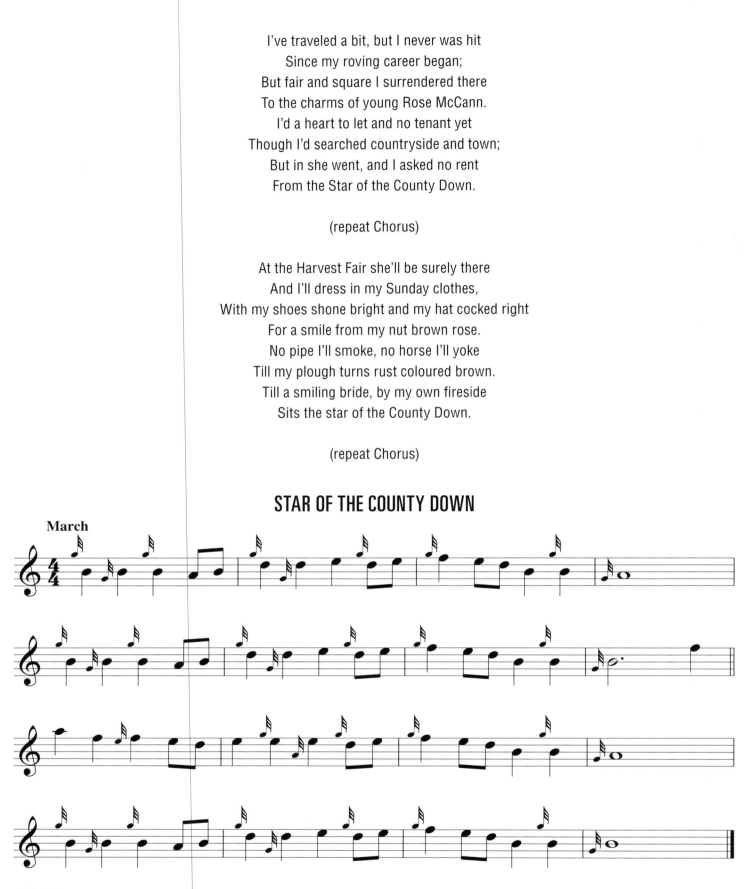

LESSON 9

Again, we have 4/4 time with only grace notes and strikes for embellishments. Be very deliberate with your playing and don't get caught up trying to be too slick. Just relax and enjoy the music. Watch the piper's fingers and listen to how it's played. Nothing is rushed. Take your time and enjoy the mood of this tune. Play it slowly. Play it up-tempo. Either way, it's just beautiful.

Practice both "Blue Bells of Scotland" and "Star of the County Down" over and over until you're able to play both without making a mistake. Tempo isn't really important right now. Practice playing to your metronome to ensure your tempo is steady. When you feel confident enough, proceed to the next lesson!

OUR THIRD TUNE — "AULD LANG SYNE"

The origin of "Auld Lang Syne" (which means "old long since") is perhaps lost in the mist of time; however, researchers agree that the great Scottish poet Robert Burns brought forward both the verse and melody that we know today. In a letter dated 1788 to Mrs. Agnes Dunlop, he praised the "heaven-inspired poet who composed this glorious fragment" and wrote further of the "fire of native genius" within.

Guy Lombardo grew up in London, Ontario and heard the song being sung by Scottish immigrants. He would later arrange the words and music that became a New Year celebration tradition.

Auld Lang Syne

Should auld acquaintance be forgot
And never brought to mind?
Should auld acquaintance be forgot,
And auld lang syne?

Chorus:
For auld lang syne, my jo,
For auld lang syne,
We'll tak' a cup o' kindness yet,
For auld lang syne.

And surely ye'll be your pint-stoup,
And surely I'll be mine;
And we'll tak' a cup o' kindness yet,
For auld lang syne.

(repeat Chorus)

We twa hae run about the braes,
And pou'd the gowans fine;
But we've wander'd mony a weary fit,
Sin' auld lang syne.

(repeat Chorus)

We twa hae paidl'd in the burn,
Frae morning sun till dine;
But seas between us braid hae roar'd.
Sin' auld lang syne.

(repeat Chorus)

And there's a hand, my trusty fiere!
And gie's a hand o' thine!
And we'll tak' a right gud-wellie waught,
For auld lang syne.

(repeat Chorus)

We haven't yet talked about certain note values and other aspects of interpreting staff notation. We'll do that as we work through this tune. If you're not sure of the melody, search on the Internet or otherwise find a recording. It will help to "sing" the song in your mind while you're playing it with your fingers.

In tunes with a slower tempo, like "Auld Lang Syne," the touch is modestly slower and more pronounced, creating an echo. The effect is stirring. Later on we'll play the same embellishment within a more up-tempo tune where the effect is more dramatic.

Before we play "Auld Lang Syne," let's sing the first section of the tune and tap out the rhythm. Your "taps" should be a steady 1, 2, 3, 4 per measure. When you see the "&" sign, this indicates that the note occurs halfway between beats. If you're tapping your fingers on a desktop, the "&" should occur at the top of your motion. We call this the "upbeat."

You'll see more dotted notes used in this song as well, particularly dotted quarter notes, which last one and a half beats. Generally, these dotted notes are followed by a shortened note (in this case, eighth notes) creating a skipping rhythm referred to as "dot and cut." Note that the numbers above the staff are exactly where the beat should be when playing.

AULD LANG SYNE

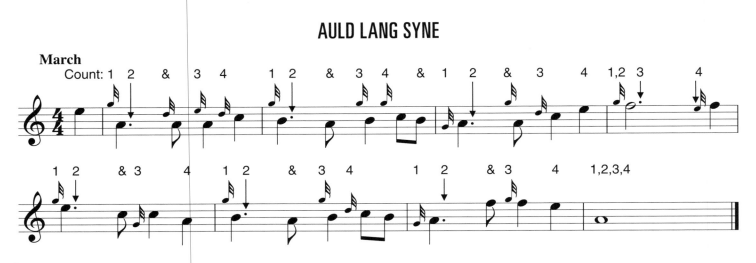

In the first measure is a *pickup note*. In this case, the pickup note starts the tune on beat 4. Now let's play the full version of "Auld Lang Syne."

AULD LANG SYNE

As you can see in the notation, we have a dotted half note in the last measure. This means we hold the note, a low A, for three beats. Why do we have only three beats in the last measure? That's because of the pickup note at the beginning of the song. This is typical of many different types of music and lends itself to phrasing and the forward motion of the tune.

Here's the tune played on a practice chanter. Follow along with the staff notation to get used to reading the notes and hearing the music. Now try the tune yourself. Take things slowly at first. Refer back to this video frequently.

LESSON 10

Wow! Wasn't that a rush! You've only been at this a short while and already you've learned three tunes. This bagpipe thing is a breeze! Well, not really. It's actually very difficult and we've got a lot of learning ahead of us!

"When do I get to play the bagpipe?" Well, just about any time you want. There's really no advantage to waiting. There is such a huge leap from the practice chanter to the bagpipe that I encourage my students to purchase a bagpipe just as soon as they're certain that this is something they want to pursue. Let's try a few more tunes before we discuss the complexities of buying a bagpipe.

SONGS & TUNES

If you're singing the words, it's a song. If you're playing the music on the bagpipe, it's a tune!

MORE TUNES

We're going to look at a 4/4 march next. The goal here is to provide you with several simple tunes that will help you to build a solid foundation for future learning.

 On the left is the D strike embellishment; it is seen in measure 8 and the last measure of "Lt. Mark Weigel." The example on the right shows how I will take the D strike apart to help teach it to you on Video Lesson 11.

LESSON 11

Play a G grace note on D. Now quickly close the appropriate note-holes on the chanter to sound low G and then open it again to sound D. This is the strike and it is played with a striking action. Practice these two distinct movements over and over. Do it slowly, deliberately, separately, and distinctly. Gradually bring the two movements closer together, but never allow them to overlap. It's best to refer to Video Lesson 11 for the correct technique.

Now let's look at the tune and again refer to Video Lesson 11. Follow the notation while listening to the music. To get started, follow the numbers (the count) above the first line of music. They will help you to understand where each beat falls. Note that "1 e & a" is the way we count, or subdivide, sixteenth notes. Just like you count eighth notes with "1 & 2 & 3 & 4 &," we must divide this count further for sixteenth notes by adding an "e" and "a." Try to play along with the video. Finally, turn the video off and play the tune on your own!

LT. MARK WEIGEL

That's not bad! Now we're going to take what we've learned and apply it to a tune that I'm certain you're familiar with, "Amazing Grace."

AMAZING GRACE

I slipped in an embellishment called the *double high A*. If you look at the sequence of the notes below, you'll see a high A grace note followed by a high G grace note followed by the high A melody note. This is one of the simplest doublings to play. A *doubling* involves two grace notes preceding a melody note, and includes a grace note at the same pitch as the melody note (thereby doubling the melody note). All you're doing is playing high A and then brushing your thumb over the high A note-hole to briefly sound high G.

LESSON 12

Video Lesson 12 is all about "Amazing Grace." Note that the time signature is 3/4, which means there are three beats to the measure and the quarter note gets one beat!

Remember, when you have two or more notes coupled together, the beat falls on the first note. In "Amazing Grace," we have essentially two different couplings of notes. One has two eighth notes coupled together, sharing the beat equally. The other coupling has an eighth note coupled with two sixteenth notes. The eighth note gets half the beat with the other half of the beat shared by the two sixteenth notes.

PLAYING TIPS

Crossing noises occur when fingers are raised and lowered on the chanter slightly out of sequence. Let's take the transition between D and E. If you hear a "blip" in between the two notes, slow everything down. You'll hear that you're actually playing D – Low A – E, which is something you don't want to do! Practice the transition between D and E slowly and carefully until you get it right.

Everyone is always concerned about what is the correct BPM (**B**eats **P**er **M**inute, or tempo) to play a tune at. Stop! Tempo is secondary to playing it at a *steady* tempo. Practice your music at different tempos to develop greater overall discipline and control. The goal is accuracy and maintaining a steady tempo.

BUYING A BAGPIPE

We talked earlier about the right time to buy a bagpipe. This is a good place to start thinking about it. Here's why: the transition from the practice chanter to a bagpipe is huge. Initially, the instrument is very difficult to manage, although we are going to prescribe a technique here that will greatly assist those who persevere. The earlier you start developing skills on the bagpipe, the easier it is to transfer what you've learned on the practice chanter over to the full instrument.

First of all, we're talking about the Great Highland Bagpipe. There are literally hundreds of variations of instruments that fall under the generic heading of bagpipe, however there is only one such instrument that evolved within the highlands of Scotland. This instrument is unique in design, appearance, and sound. It is comprised of two tenor drones and a bass drone which produce a background harmony, while the melody is produced on a chanter, all of which are attached to a bag. The bag acts as a reservoir for air that feeds into the various reeds producing the sounds.

It is important to understand that not all bagpipes are created equally. Some are better suited as wall decorations than musical instruments. If you want an instrument that will sound and behave as it should, expect to spend at least $1,000. Unfortunately, price does not determine quality, so there is much to learn before making a purchase.

Let's start by understanding the names of the various parts of the bagpipe. Refer to the image below. The bagpipe pictured is made from Cocobolo (exotic hardwood from Mexico), cast sterling silver, and elephant ivory. This bagpipe costs about $7,500 and is a "legacy" bagpipe. It is not an appropriate "first" bagpipe.

THE GREAT HIGHLAND BAGPIPE AND ITS PARTS

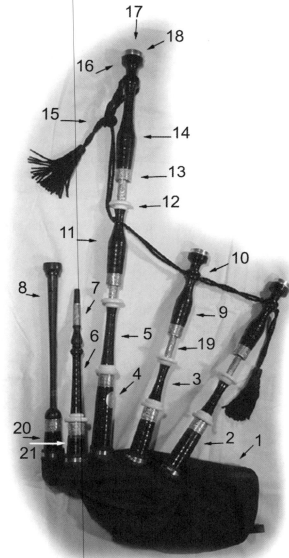

1. pipe bag
2. tenor stock
3. tenor bottom section
4. bass stock
5. bass bottom section
6. blowpipe
7. mouthpiece
8. chanter
9. tenor top section
10. cord beads
11. bass mid section
12. ivory projecting mount
13. silver ferrule
14. bass top section
15. cords
16. bell
17. bush
18. cap or ring
19. tuning pin with sleeve
20. chanter stock
21. blowpipe stock

Reputable retailers and bagpipe makers can be found around the globe. I encourage beginners to do research online or otherwise when making their initial purchase. I prefer makers from North America and Great Britain over those found elsewhere, although as in all matters, there are exceptions. I strongly encourage beginners to purchase a bagpipe made from Delrin, a very dense and durable plastic. These bagpipes come in a range of styles and are not easily distinguished in sight and in sound from more expensive bagpipes made from exotic hardwoods.

The advantage of Delrin is that it is extremely durable and will withstand considerable abuse without sustaining damage. It remains unchanged in extreme weather conditions, where wood bagpipes are susceptible and damage is probable. Other than the reeds and bag, Delrin instruments are virtually maintenance-free. With the proper set-up, the sound and performance is equal to all but the very finest (and most expensive) bagpipes. I know many pipers that maintain a Delrin bagpipe specifically for parades and foul weather performances. Dunbar Bagpipes in Canada pioneered the use of Delrin in the manufacture of bagpipes. McCallum Bagpipes in Scotland has recently introduced a line of Delrin bagpipes.

I'm going to set the bagpipe up according to my own personal preferences. This takes into account that the set-up is for a beginner. Simplicity, durability, performance, and ease of operation are paramount in all my choices.

The Bag

I prefer a bag that will allow internal access by means of a zipper. There are a number of synthetic, natural hide, or hybrid material bags with this feature. Various internal moisture control systems can be installed, which may be critical to the sound and performance of the reeds. I prefer the "feel" of a natural (hide) bag, however, this is my personal preference. Regardless of the material, a quality bag should perform its required function for several years.

Drone Reeds

Drone reed choices range from traditional cane reeds to highly sophisticated fiberglass and carbon fiber reeds. Reeds are compared on the basis of their sound, air efficiency, stability, ease of adjustment, and their tolerance to moisture and temperature.

As I said, there are many drone reed choices. Some pipers mix and match drone reeds to get the sound they prefer. Cane is the standard for sound, however, it takes an experienced piper to select, adjust, and manage cane reeds.

Chanter

Most bagpipe makers will provide their own chanter when you purchase their bagpipe. For beginners, this should suffice. When playing with other pipers (as in a band), because different makes of chanters will sound and perform differently, it is critical that all pipers play the same chanter. I prefer a chanter that is stable and forgiving of unsteady blowing. Individual notes should require little or no adjustment in order to achieve an appropriate pitch and true scale. The chanter should also accept a wide range of chanter reeds with equal success.

Chanter Reeds

There are so many good choices here. Again, I prefer makers in North America, Great Britain, and Australia/New Zealand. Purchase reeds from an experienced retailer. Follow the maker's instructions for breaking in and adjusting the reed. A good reed will last months, if not years, with proper care. By the same token, a mishandled reed will fail within minutes.

PLAYING THE BAGPIPE

The scope of this method covers only the fundamentals of the bagpipe chanter. However, I start all my students with a full set of bagpipes, but with the drones shut off. This is accomplished by either putting rubber corks into the bushing (top) of the drones or by shutting down the reeds. Reeds can be shut down by adjusting the bridle to completely close the tongue onto the reed body.

With the drones shut off, the student will play the bagpipe with only the chanter taking air. Although it doesn't seem so at first, this makes the bagpipe much easier to blow. During the first couple of weeks gradually increase the time spent blowing the bagpipe. You will find that your strength and endurance will increase as muscles respond to this new task. You'll find early fatigue in your mouth muscles, your stomach muscles, and your back muscles. The goal at first is to make a sound. Resist making the chanter reed overly weak. If a personal bagpipe instructor is unavailable, visit online sites and forums. There is a plethora of good information and good people who will be more than happy to help. Practice playing the scale until you can navigate up and down the chanter without difficulty. Make sure your chanter is sounding throughout this exercise. If the chanter cuts out or squeals, this is an indication of uneven blowing. The ultimate goal is for your bagpipe to produce a constant sound without any rise or fall in pitch.

After a week or two of this you'll want to try one drone. Understand that the bagpipe will be harder to blow as air now has somewhere else to escape. Seek help when setting up your drone reed. You want it to be as air-efficient as possible while sustaining a steady sound. Adjusting the drone reed to match the strength of your chanter reed is required.

From that point, it is simply a matter of building strength and stamina. It's not about how hard you blow, although that's what it seems at first. It's about your control over the instrument, that is, your ability to blow and squeeze to produce a steady tone.

MORE EMBELLISHMENTS & TUNES

Let's learn "Scot's Wha Ha'e." The full name of this tune is "Scot's Wha Ha'e Wi' Wallace," which means, "Scots who have with Wallace bled," referring to the great Scottish patriot William Wallace. His story, albeit through the eyes of Hollywood, was told in the movie *Braveheart*. The tune is also sometimes called "Bruce's Address," in reference to Robert the Bruce's address to his troops at Bannockburn in 1314.

"Scot's Wha Ha'e" is a very emotional lament when played slowly and with feeling. Practice the tune one or two bars at a time, repeating each measure until your fingers develop a "memory" for the tune. This is a great example of a dot and cut rhythm.

SCOT'S WHA HA'E

Go to Video Lesson 13 for "Scot's Wa Ha'e."

LESSON 13

Up to this point in time we've only seen a few simple embellishments. It is extremely important that you continue to practice exercises that will build your competence and confidence. Remember that all of these embellishments are to be played with some conviction while maintaining a steady tempo. When lifting your fingers off the chanter, make sure they clear the chanter. In order to get a clean, crisp grace note or strike, place increased emphasis on returning the finger to the chanter. In other words, lift your fingers and hammer in the grace note!

Here's a new embellishment for you. It's called a *double high G*. It's shown here as it appears in "Scot's Wae Ha'e." In sequence, play E to F, then go to high G. Now quickly tap your top hand index finger onto the chanter to briefly sound F, before returning to high G. This is a very beautiful doubling when played correctly and it's not too difficult.

PRACTICE TIP

The best way to learn a new tune is to tackle it one bar at a time. Go over the first bar a few times to get the feel of it. Then go on to the second bar. Again, go over it a few times to lay down the "muscle memory." Now link them together and play the first two bars. Easy, eh?

We're going to continue on our path of learning new embellishments and immediately use them in traditional tunes.

LESSON 14 Our next tune is "Robin Adair." Refer to Video Lesson 14. We'll also include lessons for a couple of new embellishments.

"Robin Adair" is always one of the first tunes we teach to beginners. Why? Well, it's a simple tune with lots of repeated measures; in fact, look at the first two measures. The foundation of the tune is built on the scale starting from low A! You'll also find a run-down from high A in a couple of places. This helps make "Robin Adair" a quintessential tune for beginners!

ROBIN ADAIR

In order to play the next tune you'll need a combination of notes involving G, D, and E grace notes. The combination begins with a B doubling, which looks like the example to the right. Breaking down the individual notes, you'll play a G grace note on a very short B followed by a D grace note on the melody note, which is a B. This is why we call it a B doubling or double B.

In the next tune, we'll play a B doubling followed by an E grace note on low A, as shown in the example to the left. As with everything we do, each note is played separately, distinctly, and sequentially. The G grace note is played exactly on the beat, quickly followed by the D grace note, all on B. The E grace note on low A occurs on the next beat. Allowing for some musical interpretation, you can "expand" or "open" the B doubling just a bit and then play the E grace note on low A, making for quite an effective, and musical, G–D–E combination.

LESSON 15 The doubling of E is arguably the most beautiful of all the embellishments. Technically, it is a G grace note played on E, followed by an F grace note on the E melody note. Now put the E doubling into "Nashotah Road."

E DOUBLING EXERCISES

Let's reinforce the E doubling embellishment with the following exercises. What we'll do here is separate out all the components of the E doubling and set it into a 4/4 time signature. You'll see that each quarter note is followed by two coupled eighth notes, each with a grace note. As always, lift the grace note finger and place it down with conviction.

Practice these exercises slowly over and over. Keep every note and grace note separate, distinct, and sequential. Your fingers should be loose and rhythmic in motion. Do not overlap your grace notes. When you have taught your fingers the correct sequence of notes from all the leading melody notes within this exercise, it will be time to "tighten" the embellishment into its finished musical state.

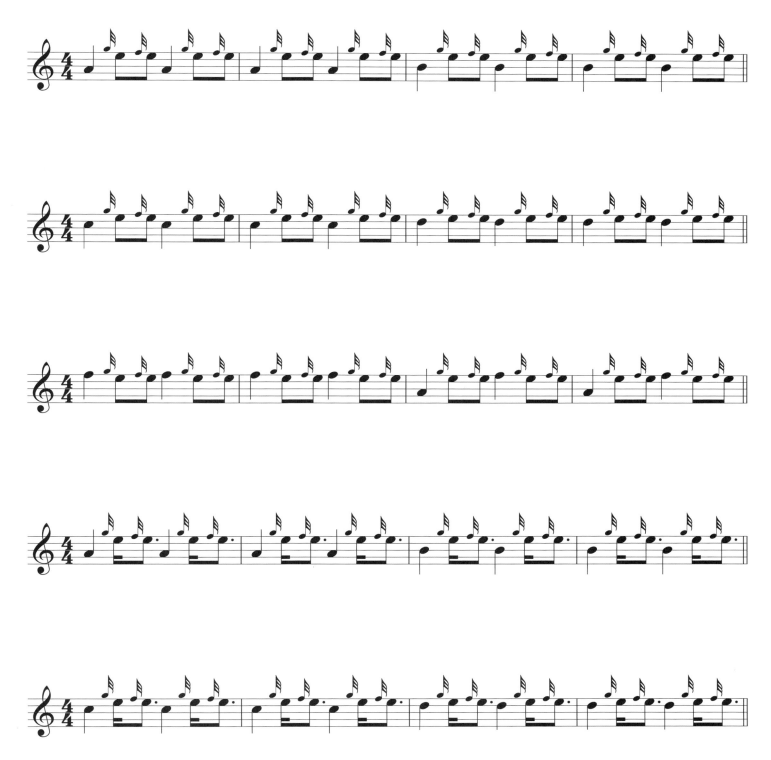

Here are a few more exercises with the E doubling written as you will find it. Alternate between the previous exercises and the exercises below to perfect this embellishment.

Now let's use it in the tune!

NASHOTAH ROAD

Bonnie Prince Charlie was defeated at Culloden on April 16, 1746. Following his escape to France, many hoped he would return. This next song was written by Carolina Oliphant (Lady Nairne) to immortalize those sentiments.

Will Ye No Come Back Again?

Bonnie Chairlie's noo awa',
Safely ower the friendly main;
Mony a heart will break in twa',
Should he ne'er come back again.

Chorus:
Will ye no come back again?
Will ye no come back again?
Better lo'ed ye canna be,
Will ye no come back again?

Ye trusted in your Hielan' men,
They trusted you dear Chairlie.
They kent your hidin' in the glen,
Death or exile bravin'.

(repeat Chorus)

We watched thee in the gloamin' hour,
We watched thee in the mornin' grey.
Tho' thirty thousand pounds they gie,
O there is nane that wad betray.

(repeat Chorus)

Sweet the laverock's note and lang,
Liltin' wildly up the glen.
But aye tae me he sings ae sang,
Will ye no' come back again?

(repeat Chorus)

With all of the more complicated embellishments, daily practice is necessary to achieve the proper technique and to keep it perfect. Exercises focusing on these embellishments are critical. Seek out exercise books or write your own. Challenge yourself to play these embellishments perfectly over and over.

WILL YE NO COME BACK AGAIN?

It's very important that we pause here and explain what we've done and why we've done it. We've explained that "ornamentation" within bagpipe music is accomplished through embellishments. Within the tunes presented to date, we have introduced only the most basic of embellishments. We did this because our goal was to teach you basic skills, simple melodies, and to transition these skills as quickly as possible onto the Great Highland Bagpipe. If you were to locate these tunes in other books, you might be surprised to see other more complicated embellishments throughout the music. These embellishments, until mastered, would present significant challenge. In our experience, within this highly condensed instruction program, melody, tempo, and the sound produced on your bagpipe would be greatly compromised as you struggle to insert and execute these complicated embellishments. We will use the first half of the traditional tune "Scotland the Brave" to demonstrate this.

SCOTLAND THE BRAVE

"Scotland the Brave" is included in the *Scots Guards Standard Settings of Pipe Music*—an essential bagpipe music book for all pipers. As you can see, it is very "busy," with very demanding embellishments. Not surprisingly, in an effort to execute these embellishments, a great many pipers will sacrifice just about everything musical and think they have done the tune justice.

Years ago, I encountered a piper who had "difficult" hands. He struggled with timing and tempo because he was taught to put all the embellishments into every tune. He was frustrated and so were pipers who tried to play with him. What I noticed was that he had a wonderful sense of music and blew a very good bagpipe. I rewrote music for him leaving in only those embellishments that he could execute within the overall context of the music. Just as an example, here is that first half of "Scotland the Brave" arranged specifically for "Bob."

SCOTLAND THE BRAVE

Within a very short period of time, Bob was standing in the circle blowing wonderful tone and blending in perfectly with far more accomplished pipers.

In 2006, I accepted a challenge to build a pipe band program within a small boarding school. The goal was to allow students a unique musical experience and to create a performing group in an incredibly short period of time. Within the greater context of an incredibly diverse and busy campus, using the methods presented herein, students would start in September of each year and be on parade playing the tunes presented within this book by November. Many of those students went on to become competition pipers, and one boy recently cracked the line up for a Grade 1 pipe band.

LESSON 17

Practice the previous "Scotland the Brave" exercise slowly, over and over. Keep every note and grace note separate, distinct, and sequential. Your fingers should be loose and rhythmic in motion. Do not overlap your grace notes. When you have taught your fingers the correct sequence of notes from all the leading melody notes within this exercise, it will be time to "tighten" the embellishment into its finished musical state. Watch Video Lesson 17 to see the simpler version played first, followed by the more advanced version from page 36.

LESSON 18

The following tune is one that you've seen already, "Blue Bells of Scotland." This time you'll see it as you're likely to find it in any bagpipe music book. This is a busy little tune, especially for a beginner. In our teaching program, students would play successively more difficult versions of "Blue Bells" throughout the year. As students were introduced to and became competent with new embellishments, we worked these back into simpler versions of the tune that we had taught earlier. After a year of this method, it wasn't necessary to teach using the simpler versions.

BLUE BELLS OF SCOTLAND

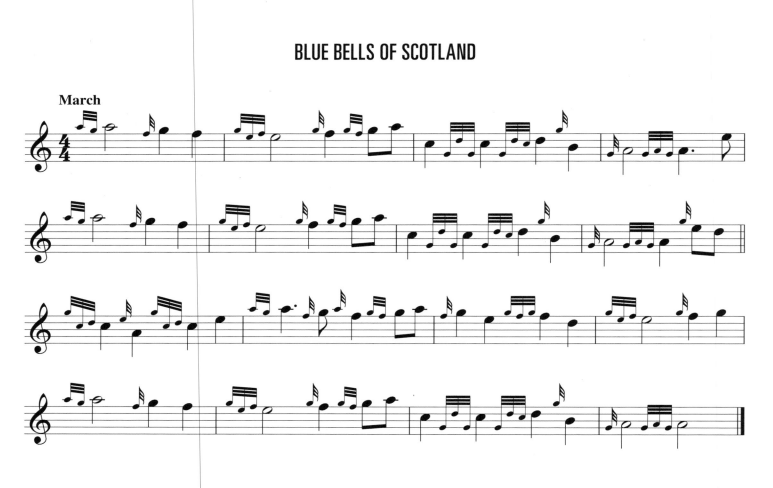

The habits you form today will stay with you a long, long time. Think about how you want to be known. Do you want to be known as the piper with bad technique? Will you be the piper to play with crushed doublings and erratic tempos? No, I didn't think so. Keep your embellishments open and rhythmic. You can always tighten them up later within the context of the tune you're playing.

Repetitions build accuracy and consistency. When you encounter something that is new or challenging, break it out of the tune and create an exercise from it. Practice it over and over until it becomes natural and musical. Put it back into the tune and play through the phrase over and over.

Thank you for allowing us to help. Good luck and let us know how you're doing.

Learn to Play Today
with folk music instruction from Hal Leonard

Hal Leonard Bagpipe Method

The Hal Leonard Bagpipe Method is designed for anyone just learning to play the Great Highland bagpipes. This comprehensive and easy-to-use beginner's guide serves as an introduction to the bagpipe chanter. It includes access to online video lessons with demonstrations of all the examples in the book! Lessons include: the practice chanter, the Great Highland Bagpipe scale, bagpipe notation, proper technique, grace-noting, embellishments, playing and practice tips, traditional tunes, buying a bagpipe, and much more!

00102521 Book/Online Video $16.99

Hal Leonard Banjo Method – Second Edition

INCLUDES TAB

Authored by Mac Robertson, Robbie Clement & Will Schmid. This innovative method teaches 5-string, bluegrass style. The method consists of two instruction books and two cross-referenced supplement books that offer the beginner a carefully-paced and interest-keeping approach to the bluegrass style.

00699500 Book 1 Only..$9.99
00695101 Book 1 with Online Audio...............$17.99
00699502 Book 2 Only..$9.99
00696056 Book 2 with Online Audio...............$17.99

Hal Leonard Brazilian Guitar Method

INCLUDES TAB

by Carlos Arana

This book uses popular Brazilian songs to teach you the basics of the Brazilian guitar style and technique. Learn to play in the styles of Joao Gilberto, Luiz Bonfá, Baden Powell, Dino Sete Cordas, Joao Basco, and many others! Includes 33 demonstration tracks.

00697415 Book/Online Audio $17.99

Hal Leonard Chinese Pipa Method

by Gao Hong

This easy-to-use book serves as an introduction to the Chinese pipa and its techniques. Lessons include: tuning • Western & Chinese notation basics • left and right hand techniques • positions • tremolo • bending • vibrato and overtones • classical pipa repertoire • popular Chinese folk tunes • and more!

00121398 Book/Online Video $19.99

Hal Leonard Dulcimer Method – Second Edition

INCLUDES TAB

by Neal Hellman

A beginning method for the Appalachian dulcimer with a unique new approach to solo melody and chord playing. Includes tuning, modes and many beautiful folk songs all demonstrated on the audio accompaniment. Music and tablature.

00699289 Book..$12.99
00697230 Book/Online Audio..........................$19.99

Hal Leonard Flamenco Guitar Method

INCLUDES TAB

by Hugh Burns

Traditional Spanish flamenco song forms and classical pieces are used to teach you the basics of the style and technique in this book. Lessons cover: strumming, picking and percussive techniques • arpeggios • improvisation • fingernail tips • capos • and much more. Includes flamenco history and a glossary.

00697363 Book/Online Audio $17.99

Hal Leonard Irish Bouzouki Method

by Roger Landes

This comprehensive method focuses on teaching the basics of the instrument as well as accompaniment techniques for a variety of Irish song forms. It covers: playing position • tuning • picking & strumming patterns • learning the fretboard • accompaniment styles • double jigs, slip jigs & reels • drones • counterpoint • arpeggios • playing with a capo • traditional Irish songs • and more.

00696348 Book/Online Audio $12.99

Hal Leonard Mandolin Method – Second Edition

INCLUDES TAB

Noted mandolinist and teacher Rich Del Grosso has authored this excellent mandolin method that features great playable tunes in several styles (bluegrass, country, folk, blues) in standard music notation and tablature. The audio features play-along duets.

00699296 Book..$10.99
00695102 Book/Online Audio..........................$16.99

Hal Leonard Oud Method

by John Bilezikjian

This book teaches the fundamentals of standard Western music notation in the context of oud playing. It also covers: types of ouds, tuning the oud, playing position, how to string the oud, scales, chords, arpeggios, tremolo technique, studies and exercises, songs and rhythms from Armenia and the Middle East, and 25 audio tracks for demonstration and play along.

00695836 Book/Online Audio..........................$14.99

Hal Leonard Sitar Method

by Josh Feinberg

This beginner's guide serves as an introduction to sitar and its technique, as well as the practice, theory, and history of raga music. Lessons include: tuning • postures • right- and left-hand technique • Indian notation • raga forms; melodic patterns • bending strings • hammer-ons, pull-offs, and slides • changing strings • and more!

00696613 Book/Online Audio..........................$16.99
00198245 Book/Online Media..........................$19.99

Hal Leonard Ukulele Method

by Lil' Rev

This comprehensive and easy-to-use beginner's guide by acclaimed performer and uke master Lil' Rev includes many fun songs of different styles to learn and play. Includes: types of ukuleles, tuning, music reading, melody playing, chords, strumming, scales, tremolo, music notation and tablature, a variety of music styles, ukulele history and much more.

00695847 Book 1 Only..$9.99
00695832 Book 1 with Online Audio...............$14.99
00695948 Book 2 Only..$7.99
00695949 Book 2 with Online Audio...............$11.99

HAL•LEONARD®

Visit Hal Leonard Online at
www.halleonard.com

Prices and availability subject to change
without notice.

THE ULTIMATE COLLECTION OF
FAKE BOOKS

The Real Book – Sixth Edition
Hal Leonard proudly presents the first legitimate and legal editions of these books ever produced. These bestselling titles are mandatory for anyone who plays jazz! Over 400 songs, including: All By Myself • Dream a Little Dream of Me • God Bless the Child • Like Someone in Love • When I Fall in Love • and more.

00240221 Volume 1, C Instruments.............$45.00
00240224 Volume 1, B♭ Instruments...........$45.00
00240225 Volume 1, E♭ Instruments............$45.00
00240226 Volume 1, BC Instruments............$45.00

**Go to halleonard.com
to view all *Real Books* available**

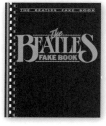

The Beatles Fake Book
200 of the Beatles' hits: All You Need Is Love • Blackbird • Can't Buy Me Love • Day Tripper • Eleanor Rigby • The Fool on the Hill • Hey Jude • In My Life • Let It Be • Michelle • Norwegian Wood (This Bird Has Flown) • Penny Lane • Revolution • She Loves You • Twist and Shout • With a Little Help from My Friends • Yesterday • and many more!
00240069 C Instruments...........$39.99

The Best Fake Book Ever
More than 1,000 songs from all styles of music: All My Loving • At the Hop • Cabaret • Dust in the Wind • Fever • Hello, Dolly • Hey Jude • King of the Road • Longer • Misty • Route 66 • Sentimental Journey • Somebody • Song Sung Blue • Spinning Wheel • Unchained Melody • We Will Rock You • What a Wonderful World • Wooly Bully • Y.M.C.A. • and more.
00290239 C Instruments....................$49.99
00240084 E♭ Instruments...................$49.95

The Celtic Fake Book
Over 400 songs from Ireland, Scotland and Wales: Auld Lang Syne • Barbara Allen • Danny Boy • Finnegan's Wake • The Galway Piper • Irish Rover • Loch Lomond • Molly Malone • My Bonnie Lies Over the Ocean • My Wild Irish Rose • That's an Irish Lullaby • and more. Includes Gaelic lyrics where applicable and a pronunciation guide.
00240153 C Instruments...........$25.00

Classic Rock Fake Book
Over 250 of the best rock songs of all time: American Woman • Beast of Burden • Carry On Wayward Son • Dream On • Free Ride • Hurts So Good • I Shot the Sheriff • Layla • My Generation • Nights in White Satin • Owner of a Lonely Heart • Rhiannon • Roxanne • Summer of '69 • We Will Rock You • You Ain't Seen Nothin' Yet • and lots more!
00240108 C Instruments................................$35.00

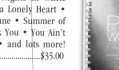

Classical Fake Book
This unprecedented, amazingly comprehensive reference includes over 850 classical themes and melodies for all classical music lovers. Includes everything from Renaissance music to Vivaldi and Mozart to Mendelssohn. Lyrics in the original language are included when appropriate.
00240044......................$39.99

The Disney Fake Book
Even more Disney favorites, including: The Bare Necessities • Can You Feel the Love Tonight • Circle of Life • How Do You Know? • Let It Go • Part of Your World • Reflection • Some Day My Prince Will Come • When I See an Elephant Fly • You'll Be in My Heart • and many more.
00175311 C Instruments $34.99
Disney characters & artwork TM & © 2021 Disney

The Folksong Fake Book
Over 1,000 folksongs: Bury Me Not on the Lone Prairie • Clementine • The Erie Canal • Go, Tell It on the Mountain • Home on the Range • Kumbaya • Michael Row the Boat Ashore • Shenandoah • Simple Gifts • Swing Low, Sweet Chariot • When Johnny Comes Marching Home • Yankee Doodle • and many more.
00240151 ....$34.99

The Hal Leonard Real Jazz Standards Fake Book
Over 250 standards in easy-to-read authentic hand-written jazz engravings: Ain't Misbehavin' • Blue Skies • Crazy He Calls Me • Desafinado (Off Key) • Fever • How High the Moon • It Don't Mean a Thing (If It Ain't Got That Swing) • Lazy River • Mood Indigo • Old Devil Moon • Route 66 • Satin Doll • Witchcraft • and more.
00240161 C Instruments.................................$45.00

The Hymn Fake Book
Nearly 1,000 multi-denominational hymns perfect for church musicians or hobbyists: Amazing Grace • Christ the Lord Is Risen Today • For the Beauty of the Earth • It Is Well with My Soul • A Mighty Fortress Is Our God • O for a Thousand Tongues to Sing • Praise to the Lord, the Almighty • Take My Life and Let It Be • What a Friend We Have in Jesus • and hundreds more!
00240145 C Instruments.................................$29.99

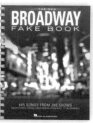

The New Broadway Fake Book
This amazing collection includes 645 songs from 285 shows: All I Ask of You • Any Dream Will Do • Close Every Door • Consider Yourself • Dancing Queen • Mack the Knife • Mamma Mia • Memory • The Phantom of the Opera • Popular • Strike up the Band • and more!
00138905 C Instruments...........$45.00

The Praise & Worship Fake Book
Over 400 songs including: Amazing Grace (My Chains Are Gone) • Cornerstone • Everlasting God • Great Are You Lord • In Christ Alone • Mighty to Save • Open the Eyes of My Heart • Shine, Jesus, Shine • This Is Amazing Grace • and more.
00160838 C Instruments $39.99
00240324 B♭ Instruments $34.99

Three Chord Songs Fake Book
200 classic and contemporary 3-chord tunes in melody/lyric/chord format: Ain't No Sunshine • Bang a Gong (Get It On) • Cold, Cold Heart • Don't Worry, Be Happy • Give Me One Reason • I Got You (I Feel Good) • Kiss • Me and Bobby McGee • Rock This Town • Werewolves of London • You Don't Mess Around with Jim • and more.
00240387...$34.99

The Ultimate Christmas Fake Book
The 6th edition of this bestseller features over 270 traditional and contemporary Christmas hits: Have Yourself a Merry Little Christmas • I'll Be Home for Christmas O Come, All Ye Faithful (Adeste Fideles) • Santa Baby • Winter Wonderland • and more.
00147215 C Instruments $30.00

The Ultimate Country Fake Book
This book includes over 700 of your favorite country hits: Always on My Mind • Boot Scootin' Boogie • Crazy • Down at the Twist and Shout • Forever and Ever, Amen • Friends in Low Places • The Gambler • Jambalaya • King of the Road • Sixteen Tons • There's a Tear in My Beer • Your Cheatin' Heart • and hundreds more.
00240049 C Instruments................................$49.99

The Ultimate Fake Book
Includes over 1,200 hits: Blue Skies • Body and Soul • Endless Love • Isn't It Romantic? • Memory • Mona Lisa • Moon River • Operator • Piano Man • Roxanne • Satin Doll • Shout • Small World • Smile • Speak Softly, Love • Strawberry Fields Forever • Tears in Heaven • Unforgettable • hundreds more!
00240024 C Instruments...........$55.00
00240026 B♭ Instruments................................$49.95

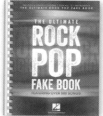

The Ultimate Jazz Fake Book
This must-own collection includes 635 songs spanning all jazz styles from more than 9 decades. Songs include: Maple Leaf Rag • Basin Street Blues • A Night in Tunisia • Lullaby of Birdland • The Girl from Ipanema • Bag's Groove • I Can't Get Started • All the Things You Are • and many more!
00240079 C Instruments...............$45.00
00240080 B♭ Instruments................................$45.00
00240081 E♭ Instruments................................$45.00

The Ultimate Rock Pop Fake Book
This amazing collection features nearly 550 rock and pop hits: American Pie • Bohemian Rhapsody • Born to Be Wild • Clocks • Dancing with Myself • Eye of the Tiger • Proud Mary • Rocket Man • Should I Stay or Should I Go • Total Eclipse of the Heart • Unchained Melody • When Doves Cry • Y.M.C.A. • You Raise Me Up • and more.
00240310 C Instruments...........................$39.99

**Complete songlists available online at
www.halleonard.com**

HAL•LEONARD®